STORYBOOK 2B

Ben and Pal

A Sullivan Associates Reader

ISBN 07-062512-3

2 3 4 5 6 7 8 9 10   VHVH   78 77 76 75 74 73 72 71 70

WEBSTER DIVISION, McGRAW-HILL BOOK COMPANY
St. Louis • New York • San Francisco • Dallas • Toronto • London • Sydney

Ben's Pet

Pal is Ben's pet.

If Ben is sad,
Pal is sad.

If Ben is glad,
Pal is glad.

Pal helps Ben get up.

Ben has to dress. Pal helps him.

Pal helps Ben drink his milk,

pick up his things,

and dash to class.

Ben tells Pal to sit on the steps.

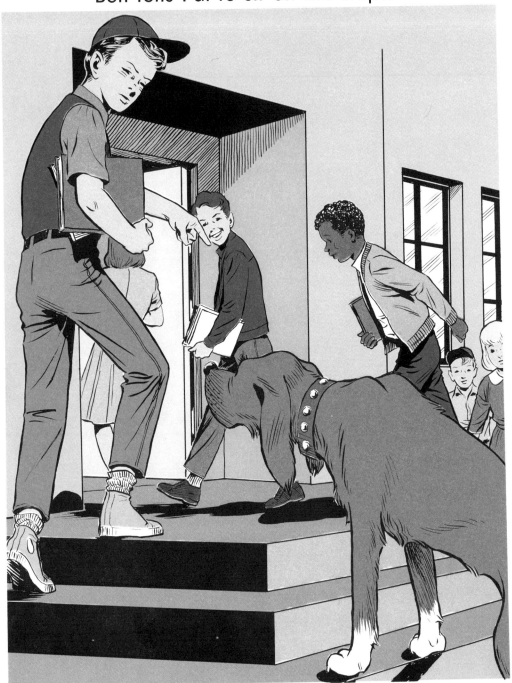

Ben is in class, and Pal is sad.

Pal stands on his back legs.

Is that Ben at his desk?
Yes it is!

Pal is in class. Is Ben glad?

No, no, no!

Ben sends Pal back to the steps.

Back in class, Ben prints,

and spells,

kitchen-
k-i-t-c-h-e-n

and adds.

Pets can't help in class.
Pal has a nap on the steps.

ding-a-ling

ding-a-ling

At last the bell rings.

Is that Ben? Yes it is!

Pal stands up to lick Ben's chin.

Ben thinks that his pet is the best in the land.

A Pen and a Pad

Ben has a pen and a big pad.

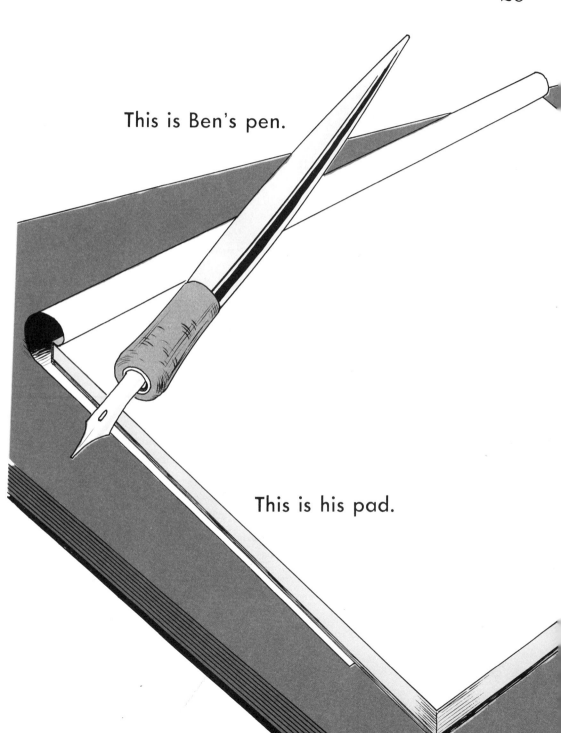

This is Ben's pen.

This is his pad.

Ben sets the pad on his desk.

The ink is on the desk.
Ben dips his pen in the red ink.

Is that a man on the pad?
Yes it is. It's a man in red.

The man has a red bed on a red hill.
The hill has a red path on it.

Is that a red chicken?

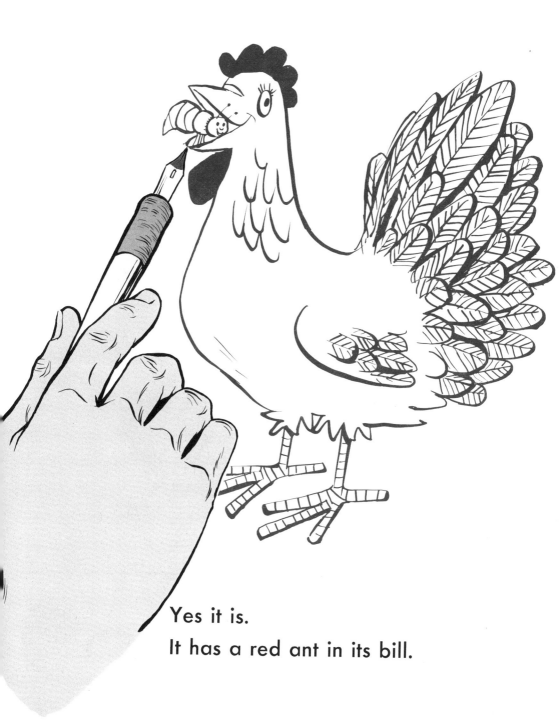

Yes it is.

It has a red ant in its bill.

The man has a red sack on his back.

That's a red net in his hand.

Ben has to nap.

Did Ben get into bed?

Yes, Ben and Pal had a nap.

The Man in Red

The man in red steps onto the desk.

Is the red chicken still on the pad?
No, it is stepping onto the desk.

A red chicken and a red ant!
A red hill and a red path!
Red, red, red! I can't stand red!

This ink is red.

Is this ink red? No, it's black.

Can I lift this up?
I think I can.

The chicken trips on Ben's pen.

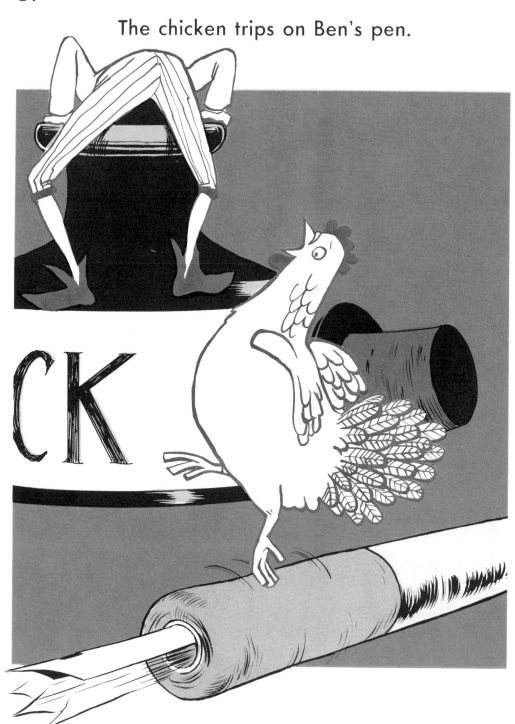

Did the chicken hit the man in red?

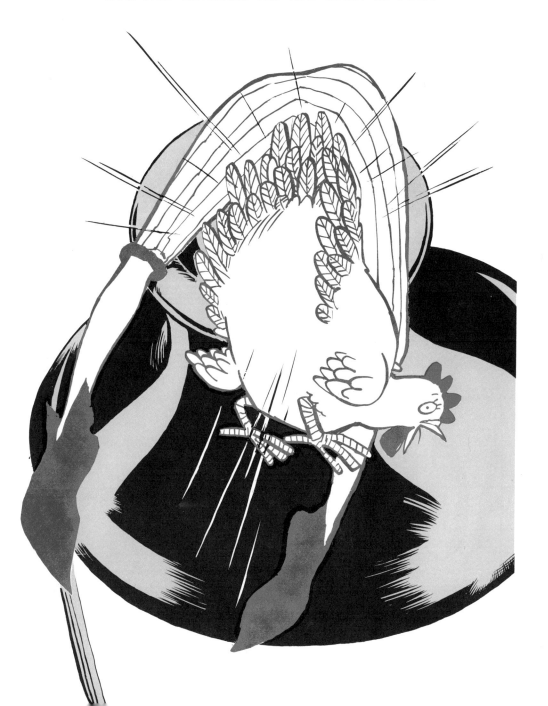

Yes, it did. The man fell into the ink.

The man is dripping. His hat is black.
His sack is black. Black ink drips onto
the desk.

Is that a rag? Yes it is.
I think I can get it.

The man can't get the rag.

The man lifts the chicken up.
It has the rag in its bill.

Bang, crash, smash!

Pal sits up.

Is that a man's leg in the rag?
Is that a red chicken on the lamp?

Yes it is!
And that's a red ant on Ben's pen.

The man ran back to the pad.

The chicken ran.   The ant ran.

The man left black tracks on the desk.

The desk is a mess.

Did Ben sit up?
Yes, his nap is at an end.

Ben ran to his desk.
Pal hid.

Did Pal mess up the desk?

No, no, no!

The man in red did it.

The man left his tracks on the desk.

The man in red did this?

Yes I did!

Ben picks the man up in his hand.

I can't stand red!

I'll get back on the pad if I get a

☐ hill, a ■ path, a ☐ hat, and ■ pants!

The man is back on the pad.

Ben gets his inks and picks up his pen.

The hill on the pad is ▢ .
The path on the hill is ▨ .
The man on the path
has ▨ pants and a ▢ hat .
His sack is ▨ and his net is ▨ .

Is the man glad?

Yes, yes, yes!